CAROLINA HURRICANES

BY TED COLEMAN

Book design by Maggie Villaume
Cover design by Maggie Villaume

Photographs ©: Karl B. DeBlaker/AP Images, cover; Nick Wass/AP Images, 4–5, 7, 8, 26; Bob Child/AP Images, 10–11, 12, 15; Gerry Broome/AP Images, 16–17, 23, 28; Karl B. DeBlaker/AP Images, 19; Paul Chiasson/The Canadian Press/AP Images, 20; Winslow Townson/AP Images, 24–25

Press Box Books, an imprint of Press Room Editions.

ISBN
978-1-63494-591-2 (library bound)
978-1-63494-609-4 (paperback)
978-1-63494-644-5 (epub)
978-1-63494-627-8 (hosted ebook)

Library of Congress Control Number: 2022912833

Distributed by North Star Editions, Inc.
2297 Waters Drive
Mendota Heights, MN 55120
www.northstareditions.com

Printed in the United States of America
Mankato, MN
012023

ABOUT THE AUTHOR

Ted Coleman is a sportswriter who lives in Louisville, Kentucky, with his trusty Affenpinscher, Chloe.

TABLE OF
CONTENTS

1

The Hurricanes' Jaccob Slavin skates with the puck against the Capitals in the 2019 playoffs.

THE STORM
ROLLS ON

The play started with a save at the blue line. Carolina Hurricanes defenseman Jaccob Slavin stopped the puck from leaving his offensive zone. No defenders were on him. Slavin had a moment to think about his next move.

It was Game 7 of the first round of the 2019 Stanley Cup playoffs. The game was in the second overtime. The next goal would decide the winner of the series.

The teams had already played 90 minutes of hockey. The Capitals had led 2–0 after the first period. They led 3–2 after two periods. But the Canes kept battling back.

The Capitals were the defending Stanley Cup champions. The Hurricanes were in the playoffs for the first time since 2009. The surprising Canes had been taking their fans on a wild ride all season. And they weren't ready for it to end.

Slavin played the puck into the corner. Team captain Justin Williams got there first. He was out wide to the goalie's left. Williams probably couldn't score

from there. But he fired the puck toward the goal anyway. He hoped one of his teammates could deflect it into the net.

Brock McGinn crashed toward the goal. The Canes forward reached out

Brock McGinn celebrates his game-winning goal during double overtime of Game 7 against the Capitals.

his stick. Then he knocked the puck past the goalie. McGinn jumped up and down. Then he raced toward his teammates in celebration. The Washington crowd was stunned.

Fans celebrated back home in Raleigh, too. It had been a decade since their team reached the playoffs. And the ride wasn't over yet.

HAMILTON THE PIG

The Hurricanes have a mascot named Stormy. He is a giant pig on skates. But a real pig was the Canes' good luck charm in the 2019 playoffs. A fan brought his pig Hamilton to parties in the PNC Arena parking lot. They were there before Games 3 and 4 against the Capitals. The Canes won both of those games. Hamilton soon became a beloved part of the team's playoff run.

2

Tom Earl avoids a defender during a 1976 WHA playoff game.

WHALE OF A TIME

North Carolina is the third state the Hurricanes have called home. And the National Hockey League (NHL) is the team's second league.

The team began as the New England Whalers. They were founded in 1972 in Boston. That year was also the first for the World Hockey Association (WHA). The Whalers won the league title that year. But they had to share the

At age 49, Gordie Howe (9) had 96 points in 76 games during the 1977–78 season.

Boston Garden with three other sports teams. In 1974, they set out on their own. The Whalers started the 1974–75 season in Springfield, Massachusetts.

In January 1975, Hartford, Connecticut, became their new home. The Whalers remained one of the top teams in the WHA. In 1977–78, NHL legend Gordie Howe joined the team. So did his two sons. The Howes led the Whalers to the 1978 WHA final. However, they lost to the Winnipeg Jets.

In 1979, the WHA and NHL merged. The Whalers then became an NHL team. But there was a condition. Nearby Boston already had an NHL team, the Bruins.

MR. HOCKEY

Gordie Howe's final NHL season was Hartford's first. Howe retired in 1980. He was the NHL's all-time leader in goals, assists, and games played. Howe was 52 in 1980. That made him the oldest player in NHL history. No NHL player has managed to play until 50 since.

And the Bruins wouldn't let the Whalers use New England in their name. That's how they became the Hartford Whalers.

The Whalers didn't play as well after the leagues merged. It took until 1986 for them to win a playoff series. Team captain Ron Francis led a three-game sweep of the Québec Nordiques. It was the only playoff series the team won in Hartford.

In 1994, the Whalers got a new owner. Peter Karmanos believed the Whalers needed a new arena. He was hoping to sell more tickets and make more money. Karmanos and the city of Hartford could not agree on a plan to build an arena. So, he announced the team was moving to North Carolina.

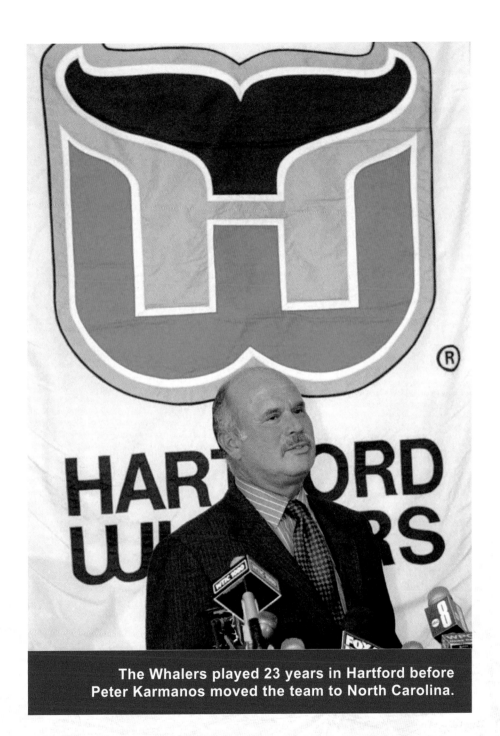

The Whalers played 23 years in Hartford before Peter Karmanos moved the team to North Carolina.

3

Sami Kapanen celebrates scoring in the 1999 playoffs against the Boston Bruins.

STORM BREWING

NHL hockey came to North Carolina in 1997. The Whalers arrived with a new name. It was chosen by Peter Karmanos himself. He named them the Hurricanes after the storms that often strike the Carolinas.

The 1998–99 Canes stormed from worst to first and won the Southeast Division. A trade the next season brought future captain Rod Brind'Amour to the team.

Former Whaler Ron Francis had come back, too.

The Canes won the division again in 2001–02. But few people expected them to go far in the playoffs. Instead, they knocked off the New Jersey Devils in the first round. Then they shocked the Montreal Canadiens in the second round. Down 3–0 in Game 4, the Canes rallied to win in overtime. They went on to win the series.

Carolina won another thriller in the conference finals. Martin Gélinas scored in overtime in Game 6 against the Toronto Maple Leafs. That sent the team to its first Stanley Cup Final. But its thrilling

Ron Francis (left) and Jeff O'Neill celebrate O'Neill's goal in a 2002 game against the Dallas Stars.

run came to an end. Carolina lost to the Detroit Red Wings in five games.

The Hurricanes missed the playoffs the next two seasons. Expectations were

Rod Brind'Amour lifts the Stanley Cup in 2006.

low heading into the 2005–06 season. But young center Eric Staal lifted his team. The Canes' 2003 top draft pick scored

45 goals that season. Carolina marched right back to the Stanley Cup Final. The Hurricanes faced the Edmonton Oilers. Carolina jumped out to a 3–1 series lead. But the Oilers rallied back.

Game 7 was in Raleigh. Aaron Ward and František Kaberle gave the Canes a 2–0 lead. That was all Cam Ward needed. The team's goalie made several huge saves. The Canes won 3–1 to win the Cup in front of their home crowd. Hockey in the Carolinas was here to stay.

THAR SHE BLOWS

Not everything was left behind in Hartford. The Whalers' goal horn made its way south with the team in 1997. The horn is made up of four horns of different sizes. It is located in the rafters of PNC Arena. It sounds every time the Hurricanes score a goal.

ROD BRIND'AMOUR

Rod Brind'Amour was already a superstar when he came to Carolina in 2000. He brought that star power to a Canes team still making its way in its new city. The center eventually retired as the all-time leader in points and assists in Hurricanes history.

But Brind'Amour's impact was felt in other ways too. He was the team captain for five seasons. For many fans, one memory stood out among the rest. He was the first player in team history to lift the Stanley Cup.

Brind'Amour retired as a player in 2010. The Hurricanes retired his No. 17 uniform the next year. And a few months later, Brind'Amour started his coaching career with Carolina. In 2018, he was hired as head coach. By 2022, he had led the team to the playoffs four years in a row.

Rod Brind'Amour tallied 473 points in
10 seasons with Carolina.

4

Eric Staal carries the puck forward in a 2009 playoff game against the Boston Bruins.

THE STORM SURGE

Stanley Cup memories never faded for fans. But the team struggled to follow up its greatest success. Injuries and declining player performances doomed the team in the following years.

But the Canes did have their superstar in Eric Staal. He became captain after Rod Brind'Amour retired. And he went on to break Brind'Amour's team records for

Sebastian Aho celebrates a goal in Game 7 of the 2019 playoffs against the Washington Capitals.

most points and most assists. Staal led the Hurricanes to the 2009 conference finals. But that was their last playoff appearance for 10 years.

There were reasons for hope going into the 2018–19 season. Brind'Amour was back as the team's coach. And the team added second overall draft pick Andrei Svechnikov. He joined talented forwards Sebastian Aho and Teuvo Teräväinen.

Carolina struggled early in the season, though. The Canes were nearly last in the conference in December. Then a January trade provided a boost. Nino Niederreiter came over from the Minnesota Wild. He tallied 14 goals and 16 assists with

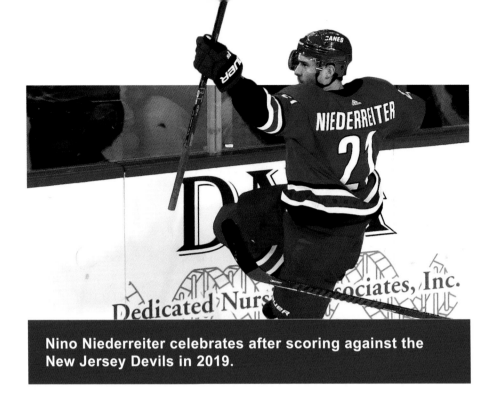

Nino Niederreiter celebrates after scoring against the New Jersey Devils in 2019.

the Hurricanes. The Canes won 30 of their last 44 games of the season.

Niederreiter scored the third goal in a 3–1 win over the New Jersey Devils on April 4. That clinched the team's first playoff berth since 2009. Carolina knocked off the defending champion Washington Capitals in the first round. Then they beat the New York Islanders to advance to the conference finals. But the Boston Bruins finally stopped the run.

That run started off a new era of Carolina hockey. In 2022, the Canes made the playoffs for the fourth season in a row. That was the first time they'd done that in Carolina. The team had young stars like Svechnikov and Aho. Fans hoped a new storm was just starting to brew.

STORM SURGE

The Canes came up with a signature celebration for the 2018–19 season. They called it the "Storm Surge." After a home win, players skated toward the glass and hurled themselves into it. But soon the players got more creative. They played "Duck Duck Goose." They pretended to play baseball. They pretended to bowl with players as pins. They even did the limbo. However, the players retired the celebration near the end of that regular season.

CAROLINA HURRICANES
QUICK STATS

TEAM HISTORY: New England Whalers (1972–79), Hartford Whalers (1979–97), Carolina Hurricanes (1997–)

STANLEY CUP CHAMPIONSHIPS: 1 (2006)

KEY COACHES:

- Jack Evans (1983–88): 163 wins, 174 losses, 27 ties

- Paul Maurice (1997–2003, 2008–11): 384 wins, 391 losses, 99 ties, 46 overtime losses

- Peter Laviolette (2003–08): 167 wins, 122 losses, 6 ties, 28 overtime losses

HOME ARENA: PNC Arena (Raleigh, NC)

MOST CAREER POINTS: Ron Francis (1,175)

MOST CAREER GOALS: Ron Francis (382)

MOST CAREER ASSISTS: Ron Francis (793)

MOST CAREER SHUTOUTS: Cam Ward (27)

Stats are accurate through the 2021–22 season.

GLOSSARY

CAPTAIN
A team's leader.

CONFERENCE
A subset of teams within a sports league.

DEFLECT
To change the direction of a moving object.

DRAFT
An event that allows teams to choose new players coming into the league.

MERGED
When two previously separate things become one.

OVERTIME
An additional period of play to decide a game's winner.

SWEEP
When a team wins all the games in a series.

ZONE
One of three areas on a hockey rink that are separated by blue lines.

TO LEARN MORE

BOOKS

Doeden, Matt. *G.O.A.T. Hockey Teams*. Minneapolis, MN: Lerner Publications, 2021.

Duling, Kaitlyn. *Women in Hockey*. Lake Elmo, MN: Focus Readers, 2020.

McKinney, Donna B. *It's Great to Be a Fan in North Carolina*. Lake Elmo, MN: Focus Readers, 2019.

MORE INFORMATION

To learn more about the Carolina Hurricanes, go to **pressboxbooks.com/AllAccess**.

These links are routinely monitored and updated to provide the most current information available.

INDEX